BLOGGING

GLOBAL CITIZENS: SOCIAL MEDIA

Published in the United States of America by Cherry Lake Publishing
Ann Arbor, Michigan
www.cherrylakepublishing.com

Content Advisor: Marcus Collins, MBA, Chief Consumer Connections Officer, Marketing Professor
Reading Adviser: Marla Conn MS, Ed., Literacy specialist, Read-Ability, Inc.

Photo Credits: © leungchopan/Shutterstock.com, Cover, 1; © Georgios Kollidas/Shutterstock.com, 5; © Rodrigo Galindez/Flickr, 6;
© Sharaf Maksumov / Shutterstock.com, 8; © sirtravelalot/Shutterstock.com, 11; © Rostislav_Sedlacek/Shutterstock.com, 12;
© Cheuk-Hung Ng/Shutterstock.com, 14; © GagliardiImages/Shutterstock.com, 17; © Ga Fullner / Shutterstock.com, 19;
© Jacob Lund/Shutterstock.com, 20; © Casezy idea/Shutterstock.com, 23; © eversummerphoto / Shutterstock.com, 24;
© Jack Frog/Shutterstock.com, 27; © diignat/Shutterstock.com, 28

Library of Congress Cataloging-in-Publication Data

Names: Orr, Tamra, author.
Title: Blogging : Tamra B. Orr.
Description: Ann Arbor : Cherry Lake Publishing, 2019. | Series: Global citizens: Social Media |
    Audience: Age 8-12. | Audience: Grade 4 to 6. | Includes bibliographical references and index.
Identifiers: LCCN 2018035588 | ISBN 9781534143067 (hardcover) | ISBN 9781534140820 (pdf) |
    ISBN 9781534139626 (pbk.) | ISBN 9781534142022 (hosted ebook)
Subjects: LCSH: Blogs—Juvenile literature. | Blogs—Safety measures—Juvenile literature. |
    Marketing—Blogs—Juvenile literature.
Classification: LCC TK5105.8884 .O77 2019 | DDC 302.23/14—dc23
LC record available at https://lccn.loc.gov/2018035588

Cherry Lake Publishing would like to acknowledge the work of the Partnership for 21st Century Learning.
Please visit www.p21.org for more information.

Printed in the United States of America
Corporate Graphics

ABOUT THE AUTHOR

Tamra Orr is the author of more than 500 nonfiction books for readers of all ages. A graduate of Ball State University, she now lives in the Pacific Northwest with her family. When she isn't writing books, she is either camping, reading, or on the computer researching the latest topic.

TABLE OF CONTENTS

CHAPTER 1

History: Express Yourself

From cave paintings to quill pens, typewriters to tablets, people have found ways to express their thoughts and opinions. Yesterday's pieces of paper have become today's computer screens, smartphones, and tablets.

What do you do when you have a thought, question, idea, or observation that keeps circling around in your head? Do you grab a notebook or a keyboard? Writing helps you organize your thoughts, understand your feelings, and explore your opinions. Although the world has changed dramatically in so many ways, the need for expression has not.

The earliest use of the word "diary" was in Ben Jonson's play from 1605.

Looking Back

One of the oldest diaries dates back to ancient Roman times. Marcus Aurelius wrote *Meditations* during his reign as Roman emperor from 161 to 180 CE. Many historians speculate that Aurelius never intended for his writings to be published. Fast-forward a few centuries to World War II (1939–1945). Anne Frank was a young teenager during Nazi Germany. She kept a private diary of the events that were unfolding. Like Aurelius, she never imagined her thoughts would be published either.

Anne Frank's published diary has been translated into more than 70 languages!

In the past, people kept their writing private—some diaries even came with a lock and key! Expressing emotions was a solitary process. Now, people feel the urge to openly share their deepest feelings and thoughts. Some limit their audience to select individuals, like family and friends. Others prefer to open up their thoughts and ideas to the world. This is possible thanks to **blogs**.

A Little Background

No one is quite sure who wrote the first blog, but credit tends to go to online writer Justin Hall. In 1994, he created a personal website about his daily life. As other people began following his example, the term *weblog* was shortened to *blog*. By 1998, Open Diary offered people an easy way to publish their thoughts online. A short year later, there were about two dozen blogs—a number that would soar dramatically with each passing year.

Blogging Today and Tomorrow

The number of bloggers continues to grow each year. Today, there are more than 31 million bloggers in the United States alone! Worldwide, a new blog is created every half second. The popularity of blogs suggests that many people of all ages, backgrounds, beliefs, and interests have a lot they want to express.

al.com

LIVEJOURNAL

is a unique place where peo
ries, give advice and exchan
unity and share your stories

Between 1998 and 2003, a number of blog-based companies launched, including LiveJournal, Blogger, Xanga, and WordPress. In 2002, Technorati launched. It was the first blog search engine. The website helped people find and follow multiple blogs. The next year, the first audio blog post aired. These audio blogs were later termed **podcasts**. In 2004, video blogging—or **vlogging**—gained popularity, as did photo blogging.

Developing Questions

Think about blog posts you have read. Now think about articles journalists may write for an online or print publication. How would a blog post differ from an article? How would they be the same? Is one format based more on opinion than facts?

Opinions and facts are two very different types of statements. Facts can be proven. (Abraham Lincoln was the country's 16th president.) Opinions are feelings or beliefs about a subject. (He was the best president we have ever had.) Find a blog post and an article on the same topic. Think about how the differences between the two writings impact your beliefs on the topic.

Geography: Blogs around the World

Putting your thoughts on paper instead of online may seem old-fashioned and outdated. But in some parts of the world, that is the only way people are able to truly express themselves. In the United States, writing a blog about whatever topic you want is largely protected by the First Amendment's freedom of speech. But not everyone in the world has this freedom.

China

Free speech is limited in China, which may be the strictest country in the world when it comes to sharing information. The government controls the **media**. Currently, social media sites such as Facebook, Snapchat, Pinterest, Twitter, and YouTube are all blocked. Thousands of other websites are blocked as well, and search results are **censored**.

As of 2017, there were at least 25 bloggers from Vietnam that were either arrested or forced out of the country.

Women like Saudi Arabian blogger Hala Abdullah blog as a way of protesting and fighting for equal treatment, opportunity, and rights.

In 2003, dozens of Chinese people who had been writing blogs that disagreed with or questioned the country's government, policies, and leaders were arrested. Over the next 10 years, Chinese bloggers, or *bókè*, slowly returned to the internet, but the return came with limitations. The government once again pushed their "campaign against **cybercrime**" in 2013. Chinese officials told bloggers they were free to blog if they followed the rules. Bloggers could cover just about any topic except for anything regarding politics or the government.

In 2018, China announced a rule stating that internet users will be held legally responsible for any personal opinion or action they put online that could be deemed offensive. When three men posted an online video of themselves dancing on top of a police kiosk, for example, they were arrested and jailed for 10 days.

Around the World

China is not the only country that limits what can be included in people's blogs. Other countries have tried to put restrictions in place, including Egypt and Syria. Bloggers have been arrested and assaulted, and sometimes face real-world harassment. Some countries, like Russia, require popular bloggers to register with the government. The government in Tanzania recently attempted to pass a law requiring bloggers to pay a $930 fee to blog.

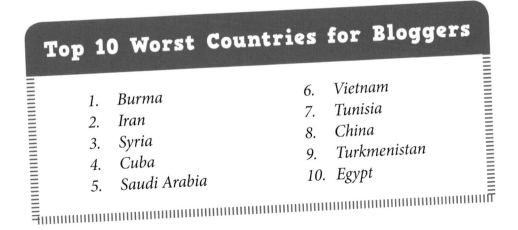

Top 10 Worst Countries for Bloggers

1. Burma
2. Iran
3. Syria
4. Cuba
5. Saudi Arabia
6. Vietnam
7. Tunisia
8. China
9. Turkmenistan
10. Egypt

Not surprisingly, most bloggers are from the United States (over 29 percent), with about 14 percent living in California specifically.

United States

In the United States, free speech continues to be one of the most important and respected rights each citizen has. The right to share your thoughts, ideas, and opinions with anyone you want to falls under the protection of the country's Bill of Rights. It means you can complain, worry, praise, analyze, explore, and discuss virtually any topic you want to without fear of the government knocking on your door or your blog disappearing from the Web. Do not be fooled, however, into thinking there are no rules or guidelines on what you can write. Even in the United States, there are writing laws to follow.

Gathering and Evaluating Sources

One of the best types of sources you will find when researching any topic is **statistics**. These are facts, usually presented numerically. These numbers can be very revealing if read correctly. Certain questions to ask whenever reading a statistic are: Who sponsored or paid for the study these numbers came from? How up-to-date are they? How many people were surveyed or included in the study? All of these are important factors to keep in mind.

Look at these statistics about blog posts:
- Blog posts that include images get 94 percent more views.
- Blog posts under 1,500 words tend to be **tweeted** or "liked" more often than those over 1,500 words.
- Blog post titles between 6 and 13 words generate the most traffic.
- More than 40 percent of blog readers skim posts.

Based on these statistics, what conclusions can you reach about blog posts? Gather your own statistics using the resources at your library and the internet. Evaluate the reliability of the data you find.

CHAPTER 3

Civics: Keeping It Legal

Have you ever stopped to think about why people write and read blogs? According to research, most people start blogs because they want to share information with others like and unlike them all across the world. They blog to teach others what they know. You can see this with the many recipe, DIY (do-it-yourself), and motivational blogs. Some people blog to create an online record of their lives and to stay connected with family and friends.

People read and write blogs for many different reasons. With free speech, you can read and write about topics you agree or disagree with, accept, reject, or question. It is essential to keep in mind that while you have this right, it doesn't mean you can write just anything. There are a few important issues to remember.

Experts believe that by 2020, there will be about 31.7 million bloggers!

Libel

Writing about a negative experience in a constructive way is common and encouraged. People want to know how others felt before buying or using a product or dining at a restaurant. Some people blog about a negative experience they had with another person or company. Venting and writing unfavorable things about something or someone isn't illegal. What is illegal is lying or exaggerating the truth in such a way that it damages a person's or company's reputation. If what you've written cannot be proven, it shouldn't be published. Otherwise, you might end up with a charge of **libel**. Remember, be accurate with your claims and have the sources to back them up.

Privacy

Many blogs ask for personal information for a number of reasons, like to opt-in to receive emails or to enter a giveaway. Most blogs only ask for a reader's email, but sometimes they ask for more sensitive information, like your full name, address, and phone number. The sensitive information these blogs collect should be kept private. Because the internet and blogs are still fairly new, laws are still being written on how best to protect people while still allowing businesses and blogs to thrive. Sharing or selling a reader's contact information with another party without the person's permission isn't technically illegal (unless the information deals with a person's health or finances). But you could still pay a hefty fine.

Taylor Swift sued a blogger for libel in 2017.

Many bloggers and businesses post and share memes, or funny images, videos, or text, that go viral online. But these memes might actually break copyright laws.

Copyright Infringement

Be sure to avoid **plagiarizing** or breaking **copyright** laws. When you are writing a blog post, do not publish anyone else's text, image, video or audio clip, or podcast without permission. Each one of these will most likely have some form of copyright restriction. While you can quote a sentence or two from another blog post, blog etiquette calls for you to link back to the post you're quoting, in addition to including full credit. Without that credit, those words (or images or clips) will look like they're yours when they're not, which is plagiarism. If you want to include photos or other images, stick to **royalty-free sites**, or reach out and simply ask permission first.

Developing Claims and Using Evidence

Imagine your best friend calls you and insists that you try the new frozen yogurt place. You might be more likely to go try it out than if you were to see an ad promoting the place. But how would you feel if she had been paid by the yogurt store to call you and say that? Would it change your response? Would you want to know if your friend were paid to promote the store? That is the exact issue that the Federal Trade Commission (FTC) faced in 2006. It ruled that bloggers must clearly state if they were being paid to use, promote, or review a product. Using the internet and resources at your library, research this matter further. Do you agree or disagree with the FTC ruling? Use the information you find to support your claim.

CHAPTER 4

Economics: When Blogs Become Business

A blog can be a **lucrative** way to earn money. Of course, making money from a blog is like any other job—it takes time, patience, skill, and hours of hard work. There is no guarantee of success, because the competition is tough. In fact, according to a study, about 14 percent of bloggers who earn a salary only make $24,000. Those who freelance blog, on average, earn under $10 to $100 per post. While 17 percent of bloggers who earn money claim they earn enough to support their family, a staggering 81 percent of bloggers haven't ever made $100. Even if you did strike gold and started making money, it may not always be consistent.

According to studies, one in eight children are bloggers or vloggers (video bloggers).

Top-Earning Personal Blogs

Chiara Ferragni was an Italian law student when she launched her personal blog, The Blonde Salad, in 2009. She started her blog as a way to express herself creatively. She never expected to make money from it. By 2016, she had quit law school (after being only three exams short of graduating!) in order to fully dedicate her time to her blog and her social media presence. She had earned about $20 million that year!

Aimee Song admits that her job requires her to appear happy and carefree all the time—something not easily done.

Aimee Song, a fashion and lifestyle blogger and vlogger from the United States, started Song of Style when she was just a freshman in college. She had an internship and two jobs at the time! A little over a decade later, she has a jewelry and clothing line, works with high-end fashion designers, gets over 2 million monthly views on her blog, and has a book on the *New York Times* best sellers list. Her blogging hobby turned into so much more.

Professional Bloggers

Professional bloggers have an average of four blogs and use at least five social media platforms to promote those blogs. One in five bloggers updates on a daily basis. Most of them report that it takes between 21 and 54 blog posts to build traffic to their blogs.

Making a Living

How much a blogger can make is impossible to say. A great deal depends on how many readers or followers the blog has. Companies will pay a blogger more to advertise or support their products if the blogger has 5,000 followers as opposed to 50. According to studies, a blogger's social media presence helps. Blogs that have over a million followers on Instagram can make up to $15,000 per sponsored post! This number may seem outrageous. But it makes sense considering that 61 percent of online buyers in the United States buy something based on a recommendation they read on a blog or other social media post.

Taking Informed Action

Do you mainly read blogs that focus on lifestyle issues? Give some thought to reading—or even creating—a blog that is dedicated to supporting a specific charity, cause, or nonprofit.

Companies that blog get almost 100 percent more links back to their website by other bloggers and social media users.

Some successful bloggers started as early as 6 years old!

Businesses and Blogs

The popularity of blogs has changed the way businesses operate online. According to a study, a small business that blogs consistently can produce 126 percent more **leads** than small businesses that don't blog! In fact, 81 percent of businesses believe that having a company blog is either critical or useful to running their business. REI is an outdoor clothing, gear, and shoe retailer. It uses its blog to share tips and step-by-step guides and tutorials to help its shoppers prepare for their next adventure. By blogging, REI helps generate a level of trust with its audience, which encourages them to become future loyal customers.

Communicating Conclusions

Before you read this book, did you have your own blog? Do you want to start one—or another one? Has what you've learned changed how you look at what you post? Share what you have learned with others. Go online and explore blogs in other countries. You can start with:

Tolly Dolly Posh Fashion
- *Tolmeia is an 18-year-old who started blogging about ethical and sustainable fashion when she was 11 years old.*

Green Fingered George
- *Twelve-year-old George started blogging about nature and gardens when he was just 8 years old. He even met Queen Elizabeth II of England!*

Think About It

There are a number of reasons why people start blogs. According to a study, the top two reasons are (1) it's a hobby, 43.6 percent, and (2) to make money, almost 70 percent. When it comes to making money from blogs, only a little over 30 percent of people actually do! In fact, only 8 percent of bloggers make over $10,000 a year. Of the 70 percent wanting to make money, 32.2 percent are looking to earn full-time incomes from their blogs.

On average, a little over 45 percent of bloggers spend less than 5 hours working on their blog a week. About 10 percent of bloggers spend 20 to 40 hours working on their blog. And less than 5 percent spend more than 40 hours. Now think about how many hours a week a person works at a normal job. Using this data and the data in the previous paragraph, what can you conclude about the expectations of blogging and making money?

For More Information

FURTHER READING

Birley, Shane. *How to Be a Blogger and Vlogger in 10 Easy Lessons: Learn How to Create Your Own Blog, Vlog, or Podcast and Get It Out in the Blogosphere!* Lake Forest, CA: Walter Foster Jr., 2016.

Jennings, Brien. *Fact, Fiction, and Opinions: The Differences Between Ads, Blogs, News Reports, and Other Media.* North Mankato, MN: Capstone Press, 2018.

Kenney, Karen Latchana. *Create Your Own Blog.* Minneapolis: Lerner Publications, 2018.

Raatma, Lucia. *Blogs.* Ann Arbor, MI: Cherry Lake Publishing, 2010.

WEBSITES

Kids' Blog Club—12 Ways to Write a Blog Post
http://kidsblogclub.com/12-different-ways-to-write-a-blog-post
Tips for young people about writing a blog can be found at the Kids' Blog Club.

Help Kids Start a Blog: Get Them Reading, Writing, Thinking, Creating
https://teachmama.com/help-kids-start-blog-get-reading-writing-thinking-creating
Read about how and why a mom helped her daughter start a blog!

GLOSSARY

blogs (BLAWGZ) short for weblogs; online diaries or journals

censored (SEN-surd) officially removed of content considered to be offensive

copyright (KAH-pee-rite) the legal right to be the only one to reproduce, publish, or sell the contents and form of a literary, musical, or artistic work

cybercrime (SYE-bur-krime) criminal activities carried out by means of computers and the internet

leads (LEEDZ) data gathered for a business that could lead to potential buyers of a product or service

libel (LYE-buhl) something spoken, written, or drawn that harms a person's good name

lucrative (LOO-kruh-tiv) producing money or wealth

media (MEE-dee-uh) a method of communication between people, such as a newspaper

plagiarizing (PLAY-juh-rize-ing) stealing or using someone's work without permission

podcasts (PAHD-kahsts) audio files created on the internet for downloading and listening to

royalty-free sites (ROI-uhl-tee FREE SITES) websites that share content, images, or video clips that the public can buy and use without having to pay extra fees

statistics (stuh-TIS-tiks) a collection of numerical data

tweeted (TWEET-id) posted on the social media website Twitter

vlogging (VLOG-ing) creating a video-based blog

INDEX